# The First Kids Book About Digestive Motility and Function

## Bite-Sized Digestive Details

GPDA

Medical consultants:
Carlo Di Lorenzo MD
Thomas L. Abell MD

By:
Jeanne Keith-Ferris RN
Genia Holland RN

Acknowledgments:
Elizabeth Gooden: Editor
Amy Chan: Layout Designer
Jennifer Young: Artist

Printed and bound in Canada
www.ArtBookbindery.com

ISBN 978-0-9813300-0-6

**Dedication:**
**For the love of my two children,**
**Jennifer and Thomas,**
**and my husband Don.**
**Jeanne, May 2009**

# Our Medical Consultants

Dr. Carlo Di Lorenzo is one of the world's leading experts in the field of GI functional and motility problems in children. He is the Chief of the Division of Pediatric Gastroenterology at Nationwide Children's Hospital and Professor of Clinical Pediatrics at the Ohio State University College of Medicine.

Dr. Di Lorenzo has published more than 100 peer-reviewed scientific papers as well as provided original invited reviews and editorials. Dr. Di Lorenzo co-authored the only medical textbook to date on pediatric gastrointestinal motility. He serves on the editorial board of the Journal of Pediatric Gastroenterology, Hepatology and Nutrition as well as that of the journal, Neurogastroenterology & Motility. In addition to serving on numerous professional committees and government working groups, Dr. Di Lorenzo has also acted as chairman for the subcommittee of the American Academy of Pediatrics on development of guidelines for evaluation and treatment of functional abdominal pain.

---

Dr. Thomas L. Abell is currently Chief of the Division of Digestive Diseases, Department of Medicine at the University of Mississippi Medical Center in Jackson, Mississippi as well as a principal investigator with the National Institutes of Health's Gastroparesis Clinical Research Consortium. He is considered among the top in his field of severe GI motility problems—primarily gastroparesis—and has dedicated several decades of his career to investigations and clinical management of nausea, vomiting and abdominal pain.

He is a prolific researcher having authored or co-authored hundreds of peer-reviewed scientific papers, invited reviews, editorials and chapters in medical textbooks.

Dr. Abell has pioneered the use of gastric electrical stimulation for the treatment of nausea related to a variety of different conditions including gastroparesis.

# Forward...

"Finally!" That's what I immediately thought when I read the *First Kids Book About Digestive Motility and Function*. Finally, somebody has written something that kids with motility problems can understand and relate to. Despite their high prevalence and significant impact on quality of life, functional and motility problems still have an image problem. Physicians and families struggle to comprehend how symptoms are generated in the absence of demonstrable tissue damage. This uncertainty becomes even more disconcerting for affected children who fail to adjust to symptoms that make them feel isolated and different from their peers. The message that often comes across is that they have "no disease" and that symptoms are "all in their head".

Jeanne Keith-Ferris and Genia Holland have succeeded where many other predecessors had failed. Their background as nurses and sufferers of motility disorders undoubtedly gave them a special perspective on these conditions. They used imagination and expert communication skills to describe how the gastrointestinal tract works in performing its most essential (and often poorly understood) function: moving its contents from one end to the other. Because they made the journey of the "apple bite" truly fascinating, the children's interest will be kept throughout the entire book. Written with great attention to detail and beautiful illustrations, the publication is appropriate for children of any age. Some of the concepts will appeal more to school-aged children and other descriptions are more appropriate for adolescents and young adults. I believe that even medical students will learn several helpful concepts by reading this book. Every pediatric or gastroenterological medical office should carry multiple copies of this book and hopefully, every child with a motility disorder will be made aware of its existence. If this is the first book for kids on motility disorders, I can hardly wait for the second!

*Dr. Carlo Di Lorenzo, September 2008*

# Helpful Notes...

**Dear parents, educators and health-care providers:**
Pick up any high school biology textbook and you will find no mention of gastrointestinal motility, the enteric nervous system or the electrical circuitry of the digestive tract. These concepts are not something relegated to the esoteric world of medical physiology, but important principles that all of us need to grasp in order to comprehend common digestive disorders such as irritable bowel syndrome (IBS), dyspepsia, gastroesophageal reflux disease (GERD), chronic constipation and many other digestive problems that fall under the umbrella of neuromuscular disorders of the digestive tract (also called functional bowel or motility disorders). As many as one in five North Americans suffer chronic digestive symptoms related to disordered gastrointestinal nerve dysfunctions. Children are not excluded. Far too often the problem is ascribed to psychological stress. For this reason, our non-profit association—the Gastroparesis and Dysmotilities Association (GPDA)—has developed this educational booklet for children and adults. We have a number of books in this series. We hope you will find them all informative.

**Hey kids:**
In this small booklet you are going to learn what happens to the food we eat when the digestive system is working properly. In our other book, *Tackling Tummy Troubles*, you will learn about some common problems that can occur with the digestive tract. Happy reading!

*Jeanne Keith-Ferris, RN, September 2008*

# Contents

* This section includes definitions for boldfaced words found in the text.

# Hello...

Ever think about what happens to food once it's chewed up and swallowed? Bet you thought chewing was enough to get the job done for turning food into fuel for the body—something we call **digestion**. Heavens no! Chewing is just the first step in digesting food! After you swallow, a lot more work is carried out, continuing for hours and hours. The digestive tract is where the real action happens for extracting the goodness from our food to keep us energized and growing. Most of us cannot feel our digestive tract working—but after each meal, it sets to work, without complaint, while we busy ourselves with other activities. For almost everyone, eating is enjoyable. Let's learn more about the digestive tract.

## Motoring Through Your Meal—Digestive Motility

From your mouth leading all the way to the opposite end (where you poop), is one long, bending, hollow tube called the gut, or **digestive tract**. It is a stretchable, mucous-lined (much like the snot lining in your nose), muscular tube that actively pushes, mixes and squishes food along its length. There is a special name for all this activity performed by the digestive tract—it is called **digestive motility. Peristalsis** is a medical term used to describe the muscular pushing of food through the digestive tract and represents only one type of motility. Motility is all the different muscular patterns needed for food to be turned into fuel while eliminating any leftover bits through the end of the tract. The digestive tract is even active when you are sleeping. Think of motility as the motor activity of your gut, always running on idle and ready to kick into drive when you eat a meal.

# The Digestive Tract Up Close

If you were very small and could walk through the digestive tract, you would see a fascinating landscape with each part looking a little different than the one you just passed through. In a few places scattered along the tract, you would have to crawl through snug passages, or valves—think of these as doors inside the hollow tract that make sure that your food moves one way through the door and does not try to sneak back. On your journey, you would discover that each section of the tract has its own role to play, but all the parts work together as a team to coordinate the digestion of a meal. Let's take the food journey!

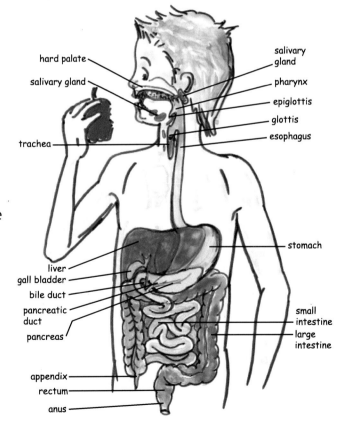

The digestive system—also called the gastrointestinal or GI tract (gastro meaning "stomach", intestinal meaning "intestines" and tract meaning "pathway")—is one continuous organ; but doctors have given special names like esophagus, stomach, small and large intestines for different areas. Having special names allows doctors to communicate clearly to others which part along the tract may not be working right. Also partnered with the GI tract are the accessory organs—or helping organs: the liver, gallbladder, and pancreas.

## An Apple a Day: the Esophagus

We can't have you crawling around in the digestive tract, but we can imagine the journey of a piece of food! Watch someone bite into a juicy sweet apple—you can hear the munching and crunching as their jaw works the teeth against the food, chewing it down to a fine mash. Inside the mouth the tongue helps to bunch up a small portion of apple, pushing it to the back of the throat—and swoosh, a swallow—and the munched-up apple begins its journey. For an adult, that journey is 27 feet (9 metres) long and takes close to 3 days! Can you think of something that is 27 feet long?

That bit of apple just swallowed will first pass along the back of the throat (called the pharynx) and then pass into the esophagus. In an adult the esophagus is about 10 inches (25 centimetres) long, or about the length and diameter of a full-grown cat's tail! When empty, it is collapsed down and nearly flat. It takes just 5 to 10 seconds for the swallowed apple to reach our next passage point—the stomach.

Does the food just slip down? No! Every time you swallow, you trigger a circular, rippling wave of muscular action that picks up the bit of food and propels it in a rolling wave from the upper portion of the esophagus downward to the stomach. This is why people can swallow while doing a headstand—but don't try this on your own—or why astronauts can eat and drink in zero gravity!

## Next Stop...the Stomach

When chewed-up food or a swallowed drink reaches the end of your esophagus, a small, thick, ring-shaped muscle, or valve, opens ever so briefly, allowing the food to pass into the upper part of the stomach. Doctors call these little, circular muscles found inside hollow tubes **sphincters** and each sphincter along the digestive tract has been given a name.

Each bite of swallowed food, or drink, makes its way down the esophagus to be delivered to the top part of the stomach. The upper stomach relaxes and expands to make way for the meal—just like when you sit down in a beanbag chair and everything shifts around to make room for you. How long do you think the chewed-up apple will hang around in the stomach before continuing its journey? Read on to find out!

The stomach's outline is shaped like the letter "J" tilted slightly on its side. Very muscular, the stomach is always ready for a workout—bring on the meal! It has the largest inside diameter of any section along your digestive tract. What that means is there is a lot of room to store food, from a small chewed-up apple to an entire chewed-up turkey dinner! When filled with food, the adult stomach can expand to hold about a gallon (4 litres)—the same amount as in a large bucket of ice cream. What is also special about the stomach is it has a valve at its top—the shared doorway between the esophagus and stomach—and a valve at the bottom—which you will soon learn is the doorway shared with the beginning part of the small intestine.

Once you have finished eating your meal and left the table to go outside and play, these two valves (remember that they are called sphincters) stay snugly closed—perfect for keeping the meal corralled in your stomach. Here, the real action begins!

The stomach, loaded up with the apple, now kicks into action. Starting off slowly, then building into a steady rhythm, the lower part of the stomach begins strong contractions—kneading, and churning up the apple mash—forcibly shoving it against the upper part of the stomach. The lower part of the stomach really does all the work of mixing food with stomach acid and slimy mucous. As the food gets runnier and gooey it ends up looking like a milkshake. The apple has now disintegrated into liquid and is small enough to be squirted past the small circular door (the pylorus sphincter) at the bottom end of the stomach and out into the small intestine. How long is the stopover in the stomach? For an adult eating a couple of scrambled eggs and toast, it can take four hours for the stomach to work this meal down to mash and slowly empty it away past the sphincter and into the starting point of the small intestine.

## Try an experiment—you will need to be outdoors.

- Find an assistant to help you with your experiment.

- Ask your mom or dad for a medium-sized, see-through, strong, plastic bag—about the size of a kitchen garbage bag or extra-large freezer bag.

- Gather up other supplies. You will need:
  - o  A pitcher filled with water
  - o  Some food items like: 12 Cheerios, 2 small cookies and 2 small crackers

- Cut off the bottom of the bag.

- With one hand, bunch up the bottom portion (cut end) of your plastic bag and hold it firmly in your clenched fist.

- With your other hand, support the top end of the bag open while your assistant pours in some water to a level of about four inches from the top.

- Now, your assistant will need to crush the food items over the open bag, allowing the food crumbles to fall into the water.

- Your assistant will now bunch up the top of your plastic bag for you so that you may take it with your other hand, again grasping it in a tight fist.

- With the bag's contents trapped between your two fists, begin gently shaking the bag up and down, mixing the food contents with the water.

- When you can see that most of the food has fallen apart into small particles, ever so gently relax your bottom fist to allow a small squirt of the liquid mixture to escape onto the ground.

- Re-tighten your hand, gently shake a few more times, and repeat the squirting.

*Now, if you were an adult stomach, you would need to keep this up for about four hours in order to completely empty the contents!*

*This little experiment illustrates in a basic way how your stomach mixes and releases the slurry of broken-down food. In order to help break down food, the stomach generates close to half a gallon or 1.5 litres of stomach juice every day.*

# From Food to Fuel for the Body: the Small Intestine

It may be called small but what the small intestine does for digesting our food is BIG! It is the next passage point for our apple mix. Just like the stomach, the small intestine has its own special role to play. The job of the small intestine is not to try to break down the meal to smaller bits—that has already been taken care of by the stomach. Instead, the small intestine extracts all the energy and vitamins from the food we eat and passes these nutrients across its walls and on into blood vessels where our bodies can use the energy. It's a very important

job which cannot be rushed! Connected by a little tube to the top of the small intestine, the

pancreas and gallbladder—our helping organs of digestion—add more digestive juices to

neutralize the strong acid that was just dumped in with the apple mixture by the stomach.

For two hours our apple mixture is slowly squeezed back and forth—one slosh back and two

sloshes forward! If you were tiny enough to be sitting inside the small intestine, you would

see what looks like the grass on your lawn sticking out from the walls of the small intestine.

Called **villi** (singular, villus), each blade-like projection provides extra surface area to be

coated by the apple milkshake insuring that all the necessary vitamins and minerals, or fuel,

are extracted. In an adult, the small intestine is about 18 to 20 feet (6.1 metres) long, all tightly

coiled and neatly bending and winding back upon itself. It is amazing to think of the power within the small intestine—pushing all that liquid around, up, down, back and forth, and all the while you can run about, not even aware of the busy activity going on inside of you. When all the liquid that was once an apple reaches the end of the small intestine, it bumps up against another sphincter—the passageway between the small and the large intestines. This sphincter muscle is very protective, almost never allowing any liquid back through once it has passed into the large intestine. Well, what are we waiting for? Let's learn about the large intestine!

*Did you know there is a party going on inside your colon? Yes, close to 400 different varieties of bacteria—that translates to billions of invited guests—are teeming in our colons. These bacteria play an important part in helping to keep us well. What is really interesting is that every time you move your bowels (poop), about a half of your stool's weight is made up of old and discarded bacteria. Now you know why it is always so important to wash your hands with soap and water after going to the toilet.*

Remember we told you that the stomach and small intestine generally work quietly during their digestive work? Well, that isn't so with the large intestine—it likes to announce its presence when you first awaken in the morning and after every meal or especially after a warm drink. At these times, your colon sends you signals and urges you to go to the bathroom. And what is really interesting, unlike the other sphincters in your digestive tract, the one at the very end—the anal sphincter—is under your control, so you get to choose the time and place when you will move your bowels.

# The Communication System Within

Now that you have learned how our digestive tract processes the food we eat, we want to explore a little further and discover how all the sections of the digestive tract communicate to each other, allowing them to work together as a cooperative, coordinated team.

You communicate to friends through phones and computers. The way those links of communication work is through wires and the signals they create from each piece of equipment. Inside your digestive tract is also a communication linking system that permits the stomach, for instance, to communicate to the large intestine. Actually, the communication

network in your gut can work in both directions for many of the different sections we have just discussed. Why is this important to understand? Later you will learn about problems that can affect the digestive tract—maybe you have a digestive problem—so understanding how our gut communicates allows us to gain back some control and lessen difficulties with digestion.

# Networking Know-how

Computers are pretty amazing machines for processing information but even a computer can't compare with the communication network of our gut. It is so complex that scientists still don't fully understand how the system works—but researchers are learning more each day about the marvels of our meal-processing organ. The digestive tract has its very own separate system of nerves running throughout its entire length and containing as many nerves as your spinal cord. And, like the circuit boards found inside your computer, your digestive tract also has circuit boards, which are called **neural circuits**—the most extensive neural circuitry to be found anywhere in our bodies. These neural circuits are responsible for running motility programs and relays (reflexes). As well, many of these nerves

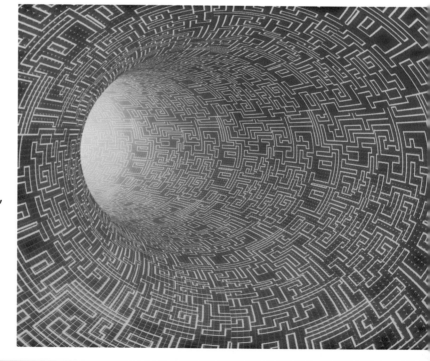

have a signaling system that uses chemicals to broadcast messages to itself or to other organs in our bodies. Our gut nerves are like the conductor of a symphony—they orchestrate the motility patterns of digestion, directing some sections of the tract to contract while relaxing other areas, all the while creating wonderful digestive harmony.

# All Together Now!

So how is it that food wakes up our digestive tract and puts into motion the hours of squishing, sloshing and mixing that we have just learned about? Hmm. Remember back to our apple. When the eaten apple settled into the upper part of the stomach, it stretched the stomach's sides ever so slightly outward. There you have it! Stretching is one of the major switches that turn on the digestive tract by exciting the gut nerves that command the gut muscles.

The entire length of the digestive tract is very sensitive to stretching and communicates this sensation up and down its length. Remember we told you about your colon becoming active soon after a meal. Well, actually it was the stretched stomach which, through the gut nerves, alerted the colon by telling it, "Hey, I just got filled up again, so you better get moving!" Not only does stretching get the digestive tract communicating back and forth to the different parts and revving up motility, but nerves in the small intestine also take communication to a new level. The small intestine has the ability to detect

## Broadcasting on All Channels!

Another very important chemical broadcaster is called **serotonin**. Serotonin is released by specialized cells that line the inside of the small intestine. Food brushing up against these cells triggers the release. Then, free serotonin drifts around until it finds a gut nerve willing to listen! Serotonin is vital for the gut to do its jobs: maintaining motility, producing digestive juices, and regulating intestinal blood flow. Over 95% of the serotonin in your body is stored in your gut. Serotonin is an important chemical also found in your brain. It plays a vital role in memory, learning, sleep and mood. Drugs used to treat depression are designed to modify levels of serotonin in your brain—but they may also affect the serotonin in your gut. That is why a number of anti-depressant drugs may cause troubling digestive upset.

how much fat, carbohydrates and protein are present in the food as it receives the meal from the stomach. Fat takes more time for the small intestine to process, so if the meal has a lot of fat, then the small intestine will talk back to the stomach through nerves and say, "Hey, slow down a little—you are emptying too fast for me!"

# More Amazing Information

Psst. Now you are going to read something so astounding most adults don't even know it. You can impress your parents and neighbours with this information. Did you know that your digestive tract generates its own electrical energy? Yup! It's true. And doctors can even measure this energy in a way similar to how they measure the heart's electrical system. Like our heart, the stomach has unique cells that generate an electrical beat (at about 3 waves each minute) that spreads outward through its network to the rest of the digestive tract and helps to keep a rhythm for digestive motility. Your gut's electrical system is always active— during meals and between meals. Even when you are sleeping, the digestive electrical network signals the stomach and small intestine to cycle about every 2 hours from a quiet state to a burst of big, robust contractions. Called "housekeeping" contractions, they make a clean sweep of any large, leftover objects—like the penny your baby brother accidently swallowed, for instance! During the midday, these big contractions are also what give you the growling sounds in your stomach when you decided to skip breakfast!

# When the beat goes wrong...

Do you know how to snap your fingers? Okay, start snapping—once every 20 seconds. Go-ahead, count out your seconds…one, one thousand; two, one thousand; three, one thousand—until you hit 20—then *snap!* Now you have the rollicking rhythm of your digestive tract! Well, you may think it is a dull beat and your attention is quickly lost, especially when your digestive tract works just fine, but imagine, if you will, kids whose digestive tracts don't keep their electrical beat. What can happen to them? Read on to find out.

As we mentioned before, the electrical beat inside your gut is just as important as the electrical beat created by your heart. The specialized cells which pulse a weak electrical current (remember, for the gut the cycle is 3 per minute or once every 20 seconds) are known as "pacemaker cells" since they release their current in a rhythmic way throughout your lifetime. Your gut muscles have pacemaker cells which are far more complex and different than the pacemaker cells inside your heart.

These specialized pacemaker cells inside your digestive tract are called **cells of Cajal.** Modern-day researchers simply call these cells of Cajal: **ICC.** The cells of Cajal are not nerve cells but are essential for the function of gut nerves.

## Meet Professor Cajal

*In 1893, a Spanish researcher by the name of Santiago Ramon y Cajal (pronounced as Ka-hall) discovered a new type of cell inside the digestive tract. For this groundbreaking work, he won the Nobel Prize in Medicine in 1902. In tribute to the man who made the discovery, these cells are now called the cells of Cajal. Decades later these cells were found to be capable of transmitting electrical impulses to muscles and nerves within the gut. Modern scientists have identified even more varieties of these cells. Some cells of Cajal are responsible for the generation of slow electrical waves that act as pacemaker cells for the digestive tract, while other types act to bridge communication between gut nerves and gut muscle. Finally, others are thought to excite gut nerves to any stretching that occurs inside the digestive tract. As you can see, cells of Cajal are critical for motility and gut function.*

Since the 1990s, ICC research has become a very exciting field, exploding with new discoveries. Scientists have become very skilled with techniques for displaying ICC networks in samples of tissue. Here is a picture of an ICC network in a tissue sample from a human stomach.

Look at the picture and see how the ICC cells literally light up under the power of a fluorescent chemical designed to be attracted only to these cells. This method allows the

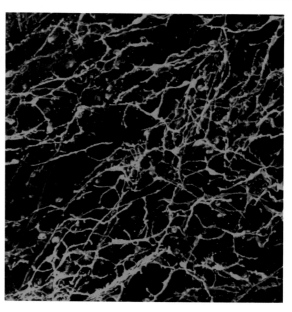

ICC image courtesy of Sean M. Ward PhD and Kenton M. Sanders PhD, professors at the University of Nevada.

investigators to clearly see the ICC cells in spite of the fact that they are within a sea of other types of cells (nerve cells, muscle cells, and so forth). You can also see within the ICC network little gaps and junctions, which, do not interfere with the flow of electrical current. Along with chemical messengers, it is the pacemaker activity of the ICCs that helps to excite the digestive muscle to contract and process our meals.

Better understanding of the role of ICCs is helping doctors to speculate about disorders of digestive motility. For instance, some children are born with persistent and severe constipation while others may fail to properly gain weight because of constant spitting up (vomiting). These problems may be related to a poorly developed or malfunctioning ICC network. As well, digestive problems are common in many illnesses such as diabetes, and since disruption of ICC networks has also been shown to occur with diabetes, it may be another one of the many complications diabetics must manage.

# Nerves Plugged in to the Digestive Tract

Our story is not complete until we tell you about one last and very important set of nerves. So far you have learned that the entire digestive tract has its own unique set of nerves that regulate its work of digestive motility; yet, there is another set of nerves tightly connected to the gut nerves, but located outside of the digestive tract. This group of external nerves is called the **autonomic nervous system**, or ANS for short. The ANS nerves reach out to all vital organs and are in charge of regulating the things you don't have to think about such as heart rate, blood vessels, sweating, breathing, digestion, and just about everything else that runs automatically in your body. To carry out its duties, the ANS is really made up of two personalities that work cooperatively to keep nerve communication signals in balance; otherwise, things could get out of control such as your heart beating too fast or your blood pressure falling too low. In the digestive system, if your ANS is not keeping things balanced, you might suffer with digestive symptoms.

# Emotions and the Digestive Tract

School exam day has arrived. You couldn't find your study notes last night to review. You are sitting at your desk and your heart is pounding. Suddenly you feel as if you might vomit! We have all felt the sensations: from tummy flutters to a knotted feeling in the pit of your stomach. Whenever we are stressed, nervous, scared or worried, our emotions can upset our digestive tract. But stress does not affect everyone's digestive system in a bad way. Some people's digestive tracts are more sensitive than others.

However, if you already suffer from a digestive motility disturbance—even though emotions have not caused the digestive troubles—they can make them a whole lot worse. Unfortunately, doctors do not have good tools to look for nerve, muscle and electrical disorders within the GI tract. These disorders—also called **functional** or **motility disorders**—are, as yet, not well understood by the medical community, and that creates difficulties for suffering kids and their families to receive good medical guidance. But as researchers continue their efforts into unraveling the mysteries of the digestive tract, better understanding and more treatment options will become available.

> ### Stomach Pacemaker Test
> *GI doctors—that is, doctors who specialize in diseases of the digestive tract—have a test to measure the electrical activity of the stomach. Called **electrogastrography** (electro-gas-tr'aw-graphy) or EGG for short, this test provides doctors with a method to determine the health of the pacemaker cells of Cajal. The test is simple. Several sticky pads with attached wires are placed on the skin of your abdomen just over top of your stomach region. The wires are then attached to a machine that measures the stomach's electrical activity. Remember, healthy cells of Cajal are essential for normal gut motility.*

# Understanding More

### Autonomic nervous system (ANS)

A branch of the body's nervous system involved with automatically regulating a number of important bodily functions such as heart rate, blood pressure, digestion, and blood flow, to name a few. The ANS consists of two major sub-branches: the sympathetic and parasympathetic nervous systems. Both sub-branches of the ANS are important for modifying digestive motility. The sympathetic pathway is thought to be an important route for signaling sensations of pain and nausea from the gut to the brain.

### Cells of Cajal / ICC

Also called the interstitial (in-ter-sti-she-al) cells of Cajal—or ICC—these are populations of specialized cells intermixed with gut nerves and gut tissue. Many different types of ICCs exist inside the digestive tract. Some ICCs act as pacemaker cells by releasing electrical energy while others act as communication-bridging cells. ICCs, together with gut-nerve and gut-muscle cells, help to create the scaffolding structure that links up a complex communication network necessary for the coordination of gut motility and function. Researchers are just beginning to understand the system.

### Digestion

The mechanical and chemical processes by which food is broken down inside our bodies and made available for absorption into our blood stream.

### Digestive motility

The variety of muscular activity carried out by the digestive tract for the mechanical breaking down of food and its movement though the digestive tract.

### Digestive tract

The hollow muscular organ responsible for the digestion, absorption and elimination of our meal.

### Electrogastrography (EGG)

The EGG is a piece of equipment used by GI doctors for the detection of abnormal electrical rhythms generated by the stomach. It can also be used to look for abnormal electrical rhythms generated by the small intestine.

### Functional GI disorders

Wide-ranging disorders of the digestive tract that affect the gut's ability to function properly. Doctors understand very little as to what causes these disorders—but stress and emotions can make the problems feel much worse. Some of these disorders may be related to the gut overreacting to the normal stretching created by a meal. This overreaction can lead to the sensation of abdominal pain. In other cases, motility is abnormal—either too fast (causing problems such as diarrhea) or too slow (causing constipation). Or, the electrical system of the digestive tract may be abnormal. In most cases, the ANS is also not responding properly.

## Motility disorders

Disorders of motility are neuromuscular disorders of the digestive tract and are the same as functional GI disorders but with a greater degree of problems arising from poor gut motor activity—or motility.

## Neural circuits

Specialized cells of the nervous system that transmit electrical and chemical signals to and from each other.

## Peristalsis

Consists of a powerful muscular squeeze within a segment of the digestive tract creating one kind of motility pattern that is responsible for the movement of food through the gut.

## Serotonin

Serotonin is an important signaling chemical for nerves within the brain and gut. Most of the serotonin made by our body is stored in specialized cells that line the digestive tract. When food brushes up against them, these cells release their stored serotonin.

### Sphincter

A small circular muscle found inside hollow tubes within the body. The digestive tract has many sphincter muscles that help control the direction of flow of our food and digestive juices. Each sphincter muscle in the digestive tract has a unique name. For example, the lower esophageal sphincter (LES) serves as the door between the esophagus and stomach; the pylorus is the sphincter between the bottom of the stomach and the beginning section of the small intestine, and the ileal cecal valve is the sphincter at the end of the small intestine and the beginning of the large intestine. The last sphincter in your digestive tract is the anal sphincter, or anus for short. It is under your voluntary control permitting you to choose the time and place to empty your bowel.

### Villi (singular, villus)

Small finger-like projections that extend out into the small digestive tract and serve to provide more surface area for the absorption of the liquefied food.

# About the Authors

Jeanne Keith-Ferris RN, BScN is the Founder and President of the Gastroparesis and Dysmotilities Association, an international non-profit organization dedicated to increasing awareness and education of digestive motility disorders as well as providing advocacy for those who suffer with them. Jeanne earned the name "Motility Mom" when her two children acquired gastroparesis following a gut infection at the ages of 7 and 9 respectively. Jeanne and her husband Don have helped to nurture the establishment of the Centre for Digestive Motility (CDM) at the University of Calgary in Alberta, Canada. The Centre, with its dedicated doctors and researchers, is working on better ways to diagnose and treat severe digestive motility problems. Jeanne and Don live in Calgary with there now-teenaged children.

Genia Holland RN has struggled with gastroparesis for many years. She is a big advocate for increased awareness of digestive motility disorders with the public. She lives with her two children and husband in Arkansas.